The Water Cycle

Steve Parker

Contents

In the beginning...

Long ago, high in the sky, there
was a tiny drop of water.
It floated in the air. Around it
were millions of other water
drops. All together, they made a cloud.

The cloud was not white and fluffy. It was
a dark, damp raincloud. The water drop
began to fall. It fell faster and faster.

The raindrop fell down, down, then SPLASH!
It landed on a dinosaur's head! It bounced
onto the ground and **soaked** into the soil.

3

Underground

The water drop moved very slowly down through the soil. It went past stones, worms and the roots of plants. It went deeper and deeper under the ground. Finally the water drop soaked into a stream under the ground. The stream was cold and it flowed very fast.

The stream flowed out through a hole in
a hillside. It splashed down the hillside
and joined other streams. Eventually the
water drop flowed into a wide, quiet river.

In the river

The water drop liked the river. Many animals lived there. There were tall reeds along the banks. The flow of water was slow and gentle.

reed
water lily
frog
diving beetle
waterweed
water snail

Nice and clean

The river flows towards the town. Some of the water pours into **pipes**. There is mud, rubbish and **germs** in the river water. It must be cleaned before people can use it.

What happens at a water treatment works

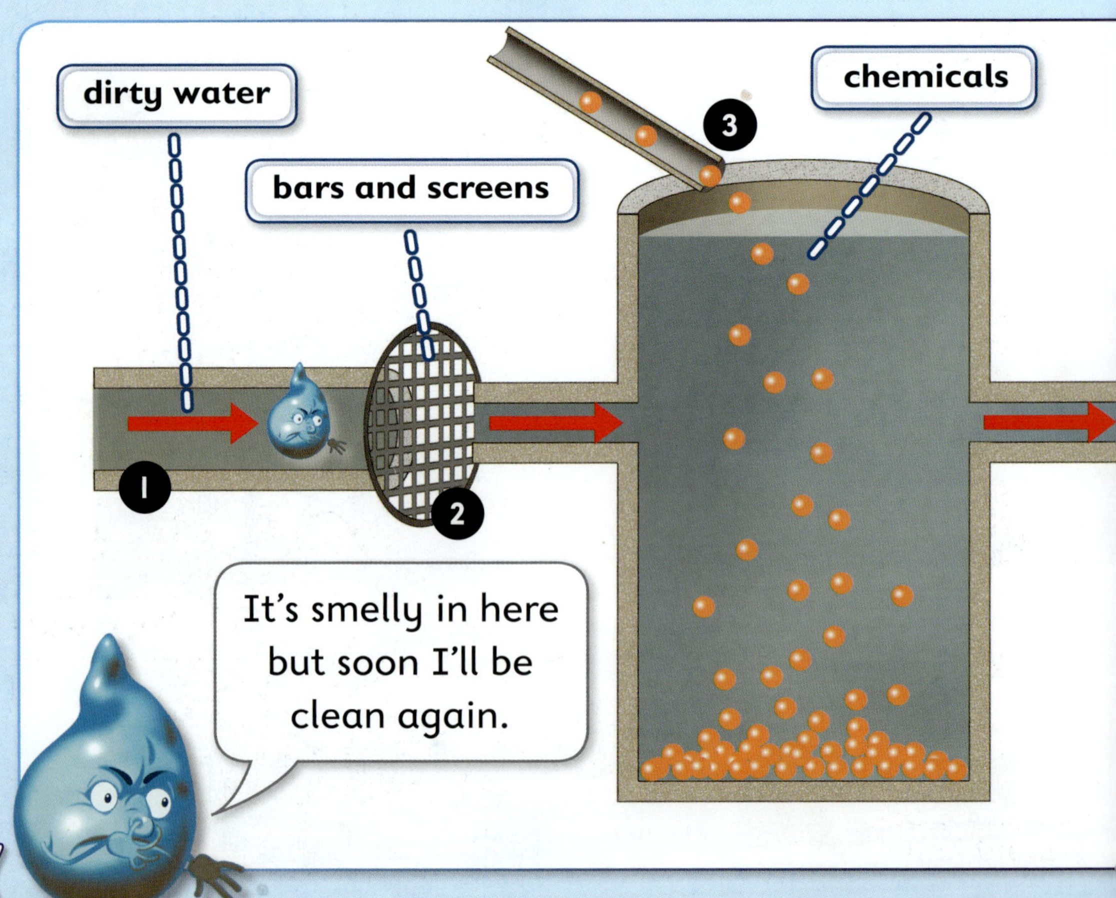

8

1. Dirty water enters the pipes.

2. It passes through the bars and screens. This filters out large objects such as leaves and twigs.

3. **Chemicals** are added to clean the water.

4. The water flows on through lots of small stones and tiny bits of sand. This filters out very small objects and dirt.

5. More chemicals are added to kill germs.

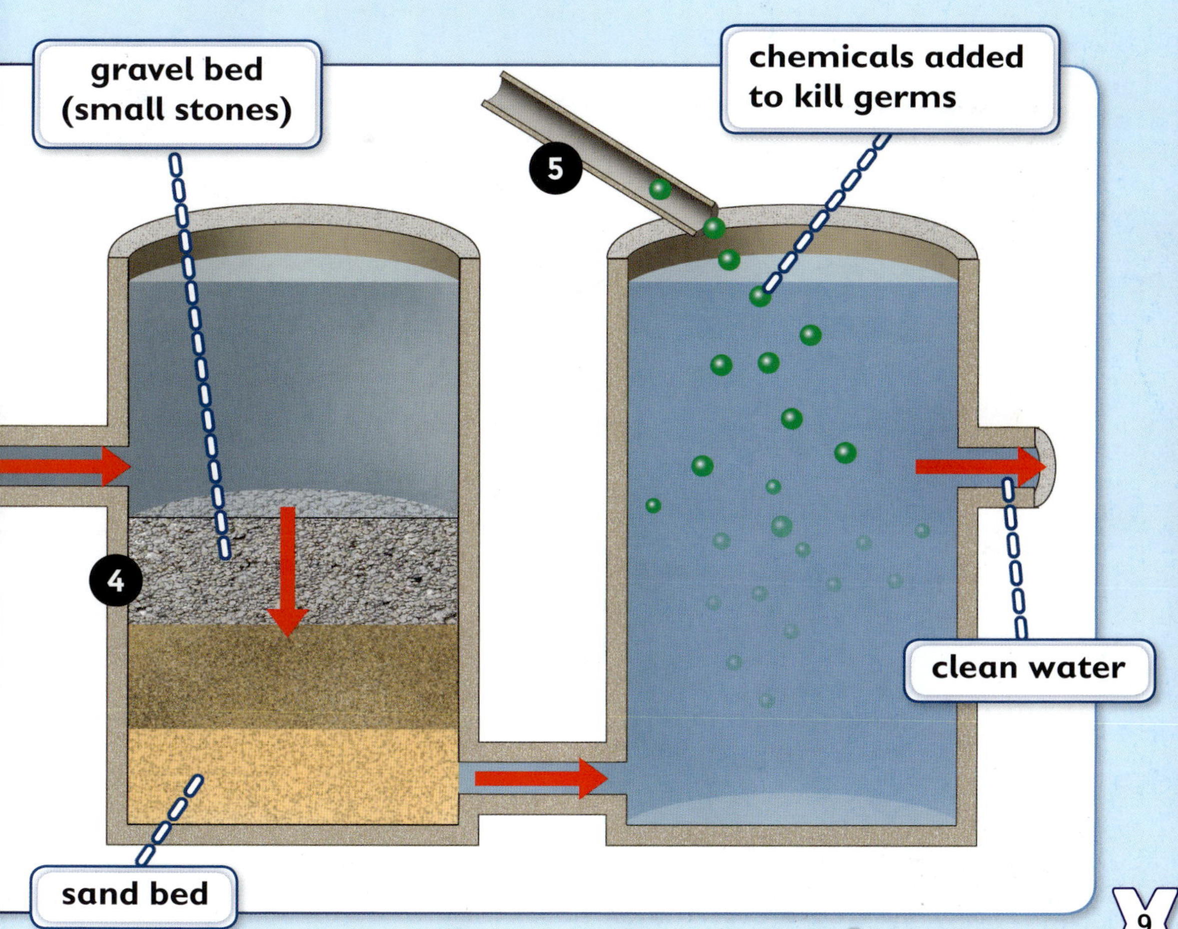

Water at home

Every day at home, we all use lots of water. Turn on the tap and out it comes. Can you think of all the ways we use water? How many can you spot in the picture?

What would you do if you didn't have water on tap?

Down the drain

The water drop gurgles down the plug
hole into the **drain**. Water from the
toilet goes here too. Rainwater also
flows into the drain.

The dirty water flows through the water treatment works where it is cleaned.

The dirty water from the drains must be cleaned. Otherwise it would harm fish and other animals in the river. The dirty water flows back to the water treatment works. There it is cleaned again. The soap, dirt, toothpaste and other substances are taken out. The clean water flows back into the river.

Ice-cold water

It's now winter. The water is so cold, it cannot flow. It becomes hard and solid. This is called freezing. Frozen water is called ice. A sheet of ice freezes on the surface of the water.

In spring, when it is warmer, the ice will melt back into water. All of the river will flow again.

Water power

The water drop reaches a wall across the river. This wall stops most of the flow. The wall is called a dam.

1. The water collects behind the dam to form a large lake.

2. The water flows through pipes inside the dam.

3. It presses on wheels called turbines to make them spin round.

4. The turbines produce electricity.

5. Electricity passes through wires to be used by us.

This dam is very useful. As water flows through pipes inside, it presses on wheels called turbines. The water makes the turbines spin around. This produces electricity.

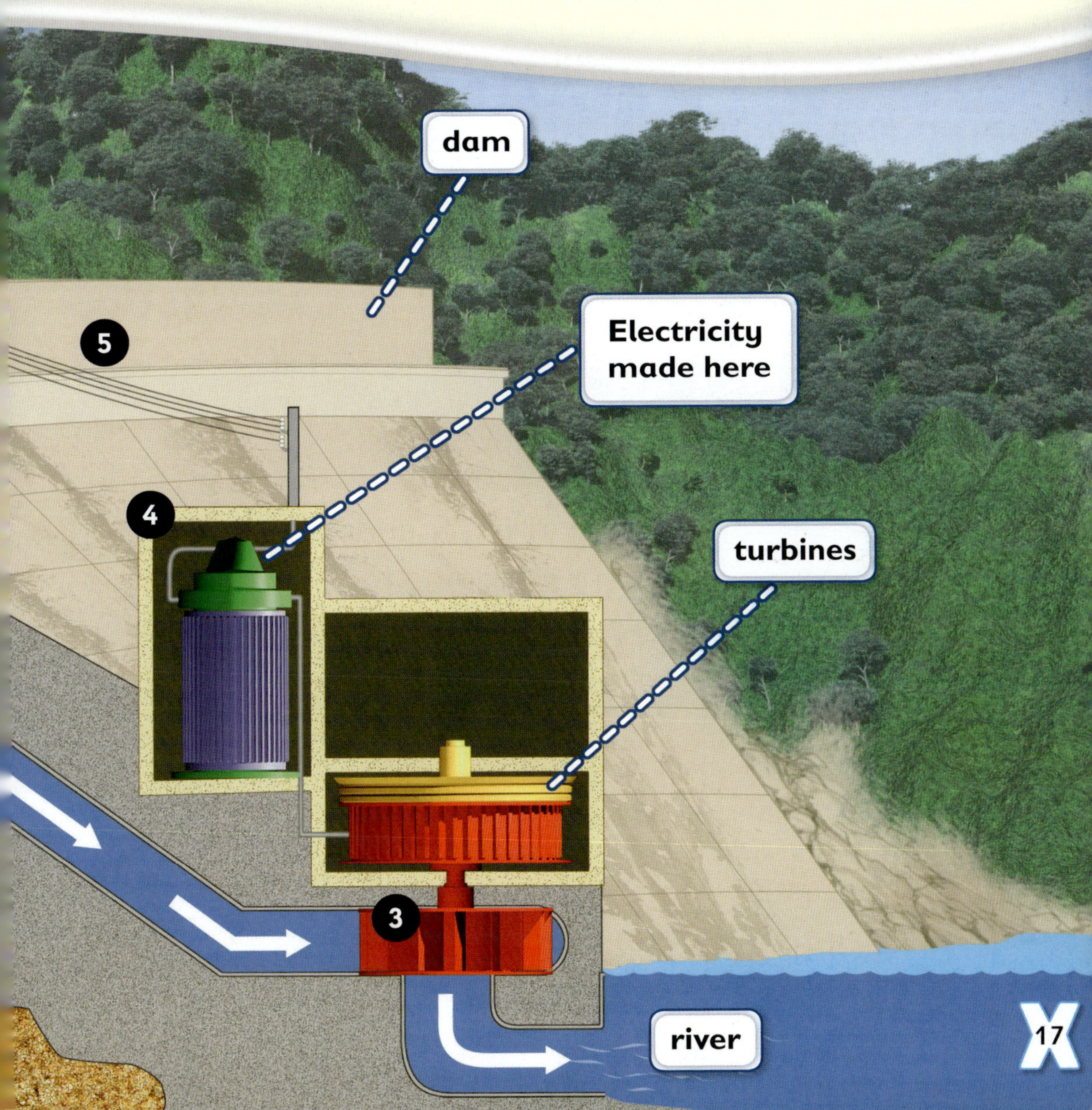

Not much water

The river flows on and on. In some hot countries the land on either side has little rain. It is very dry and few plants can grow. This is a desert.

A long time without rain or water is called a drought. People living in dry places have to be very careful not to waste water.

People dig long holes called ditches to carry the water from the river to their fields.

Out to see the sea

At last the river reaches the sea. The water drop floats along the coast. There is a sandy beach where people have fun.

The water drop floats out into the wide open ocean. Most of the water in the world is in the seas and oceans. Most of the Earth's surface is covered by water.

Sea to sky

The sun warms the water in the sea. The heat turns the water into something we cannot see called water vapour. The vapour goes up into the sky, where it is colder. Then the vapour turns back into water drops and forms a cloud. The cloud blows over the land.

It starts to rain …

Water drops like me go round and round. It's called the water cycle. Here I go again!
sun
clouds
water vapour
sea

Glossary

chemicals   substances that are found in nature or made in a science laboratory

drain   a pipe that carries water away under the ground

flow   when water flows it moves along

germ   a germ is a tiny living thing that is too small to see

pipes   hollow tubes that gas or liquid can go along

soak   to make something very wet

Index